LEGENDS OF

Louise Maskill

BRADWELL
BOOKS

Published by Bradwell Books

Carrwood Road, Chesterfield S41 9QB

Email: info@bradwellbooks.co.uk

British Library Cataloguing in Publication Data: a catalogue record for
this book is available from the British Library.

1st Edition

ISBN: 9781912060719

Design by: Andrew Caffrey

Typesetting by: Mark Titterton

Print: CPI Group (UK) Ltd, Croydon, CR0 4YY

Photograph Credits: iStock and credited individually

CONTENTS

INTRODUCTION

The folk tales and folklore of the British Isles make for an endlessly fascinating study. The cultural melting pot of ancient Britain has bequeathed us with an eclectic mix of heroes, villains, myths and legends, and over the centuries a glorious confusion of beliefs has evolved to account for phenomena both natural and supernatural, and to explain and inhabit landscape features such as hills, rivers, woods, chasms, moors and marshes.

Roseberry Topping, North York Moors. iStock

Our ancestors lived very different lives to those we enjoy today. Most were tied to the land and had intimate relationships with the changing seasons and the natural world. Few travelled further than their local environs and perhaps the nearest market town, but this seemingly limited existence was nevertheless richly coloured with an awareness of another world, where supernatural beings existed just outside mortal ken, where illness and death could be caused not by germs or viruses but by witchcraft or water-dwelling monsters, and where mythical heroes could be brought to life in dramatic stories and legends retold down the generations.

In this book you will be introduced to some of the legends and folklore which enriched the days and nights of Yorkshire folk in days gone by. You will meet fairies, hobs, boggarts, witches, giants and the Devil, and you will encounter heroic legendary figures such as Robin Hood, King Arthur and the many dragon slayers who freed their neighbours from terror and dread, often perishing themselves in the endeavour. You will read about superstitions and omens for both good and bad luck, the ceremonies and rituals associated with the rural year and critical stages in life, and learn about a few particularly Yorkshire customs.

Welcome to Yorkshire, a truly magical county!

GIANTS

Lots of landscape features, especially across the Pennines and the North York Moors, are explained by the activities of giants in long-bygone times when they still walked the land. Isolated stones (often glacial erratics) are thought to have been thrown by giants, often in a fit of temper or during arguments or fights. Sometimes these fights were with the Devil (who is also responsible for a number of landscape features), but often they were between the giant and his wife. The giant Rombald and his wife had a notoriously volatile relationship and their arguments often ended with flying rocks, as did those of the giant Wade and his wife Bell. The Carlow Stone, near Semer Water, was thrown at Rombald by the Devil, while Almscliffe Crag above Wharfedale was either thrown by the Devil or dropped by Rombald's wife.

Neolithic or Bronze Age workings and landscape features are often attributed to giants; there are a number of burial cairns known as the Giant's Grave, while Wade's Stone – a two-metre standing stone on the North York Moors, near the village of East Barnby – was thought to be originally one of a pair standing twelve feet apart, which marked out the grave of the giant Wade. Another local story associated with Wade is that he lived at the ancient and nearby Mulgrave Castle, while his wife Bell lived in her own castle at Pickering some twenty miles to the south. Each built their own castles but had only one hammer to do the job, which they threw backwards and forwards between them, shouting to warn each other that it was on its way.

Wade seems to have been a prolific builder – he and Bell are also said to have constructed Wade's Causeway on Wheeldale Moor, scooping out the huge depression of the Devil's Punchbowl in the process, so that Bell could more easily travel to milk her giant cow who roamed the high moorlands. Other walls, ruins, castles and ancient roads are also attributed to him, and he is said to have been the father of the legendary blacksmith Wayland, who forged King Arthur's sword Excalibur.

Like Wade, the giant Rombald was fond of building and tearing up the landscape, but he also seems to have been rather clumsy. He created the iconic Cow and Calf rock formation on Ilkley Moor by tripping and falling, splitting the rocks as he hit the ground. Rombald's wife created the tubular cavity in the Hitching Stone, on Keighley Moor, by jamming her broom handle into the rock to give her purchase as she attempted to heave the stone up to throw at her husband during a particularly violent domestic disagreement. She also created the pile of stones on Burley Moor known as the Little Skirtful, tumbling them from her skirt as she crossed the moor.

The Cow and Calf rock formation on Ilkley Moor, caused when Wade the giant tripped and fell. iStock

The Pen Hill giant, once resident in a castle on Pen Hill in Wensleydale, was a legendary descendant of Thor, and a particularly bloodthirsty and violent example of the giant race. He used the land around his castle to graze his herds of swine, which were a source of great pride to him. One day while patrolling his lands with his hound Wolfhead, he came across a local shepherdess and took a shine to her. She rejected his advances and took to her heels, at which Wolfhead and the giant gave chase. Wolfhead eventually brought her down but was injured when she struck him with a rock. This so angered the giant that he slew the girl on the spot.

News of this atrocity spread through the neighbourhood, and soon one of the giant's precious swine was killed. Enraged, he charged down from the castle to confront the local villagers, but not before blaming Wolfhead and driving the hound away with vicious kicks. Reaching the village, the giant threatened to kill the lastborn son in every family unless the swine killer was turned over to him. An old man known as the Seer of Carperby foretold doom for the giant if he made good on his threat.

Back at his castle, the giant was confronted by an elderly retainer who warned his master that he had seen an evil omen – nine ravens atop the castle walls. The giant was infuriated and beat his servant before issuing forth again to the village; but meanwhile the battered retainer gathered all the flammable material in the castle and set it afire.

At the village, the giant found more of his dead swine, as well as the Seer. While the giant roared his rage the old man pointed wordlessly at the castle in the distance, from which black smoke was now belching forth. Turning back to the Seer, the giant encountered the even more terrifying apparition of the slain shepherdess, now holding the lead of the snarling Wolfhead. She released the hound, and it drove the giant over a cliff to his death.

FAIRIES AND TREASURE HUNTERS

Yorkshire has a rich and venerable tradition of fairy lore. Like giants, the little folk are often credited with creating or living in landscape features such as cairns, burial mounds or caves, and there are many stories of travellers coming across them or hearing the sounds of their revelries.

One such is attached to Willy Howe, a huge round barrow located between the villages of Wold Newton and Burton Fleming, which has persistent stories connected with the fair folk. The legend tells that a local farmer, travelling home late one night, heard the sounds of revelry from within the mound. Approaching more closely, he found a large open doorway into the barrow through which he could see a party in full swing, with food, drink, music and many fairy revellers. Seeing him standing outside, the party-goers invited him in and offered him a drink in a fabulous golden cup, but he was wise to this; he tipped the contents of the cup away and fled the mound, pursued by the fairies. His horse was swift and he reached home safely still clutching his fairy cup, which turned out to be of unknown metal and astonishingly fine workmanship. He presented it to King Henry I, and it eventually found its way into the royal treasury of Henry II before disappearing from history.

Another story relates that a treasure hunter dug into the top of the mound and located a large chest full of gold. Determined to extract it, he attached a long train of horses and attempted to pull

it free. However, when he uttered the blasphemous words "Hop Perry, prow Mark, whether God's will or no we'll have this ark", the traces broke in many places and the chest sank into the earth at the centre of the mound, never to be found again.

Probably the most famous Yorkshire fairies appear in the photographs taken in 1917 in Cottingley, near Bradford, by Elsie Wright and her cousin Frances. The total of five images show Elsie and Frances supposedly watching and talking to a selection of winged fairies; the pictures were widely suspected to be fakes even from the beginning, but they were taken seriously by many people, not least Sir Arthur Conan Doyle and other leading spiritualists. Elsie finally confessed that four of the five famous images were created using cardboard cut-outs of fairy images which were later disposed of in the nearby beck – but the fifth image is less easy to interpret, and Frances continued to insist it was genuine until her death in 1986.

An image of the Cottingley fairies. iStock

Other Yorkshire fairies are less friendly than the little people of Cottingley. One night a drunken farmer accepted a bet to enter Mulgrave Woods near Whitby and call on the famously ill-tempered fairy who lived there, named Jeanie of Biggersdale. He did so, calling on her by name, but when she came charging to meet him he fled, and only escaped because of the swiftness of his horse. The creature was not so lucky, however – horse and rider attempted to jump a running brook with the enraged fairy hard on their heels (for everyone knows fairies can't cross running water), but Jeanie grabbed the horse's hindquarters and broke the beast in half.

Elbolton Hill, near Burnsall in the Yorkshire Dales, is another haunt of the little people; one local passing close by at night heard them singing and attempted to join in, enraging them so much that they drove him away with pinches and slaps. In the melee, however, he managed to grab one of the tiny creatures and shove it in his pocket. He intended to take it home for his daughter, but when he arrived there was no sign of it.

Many of the small folk are associated with water. The Queen of the Fairies is said to live behind Janet's Foss, a waterfall near Malham, and they are known to wash their clothes in Claymore Well near Kettleness, and bathe in the bath house in the White Wells Spa café on the edge of Ilkley Moor.

Fairies are often accused of stealing human children and leaving changelings in their place, who may be known by their unhealthiness, small and crooked stature and general grumpiness of outlook. One unfortunate farmer near Almscliffe Crag in Wharfedale claimed to have had three of his eight children stolen by fairies and replaced by changelings; the human five were handsome, strong and cheerful, but the other three were weak,

Janet's Foss waterfall. Mark Titterton

Beautiful Wharfedale. iStock

afflicted and possessed of spectacularly bad temper. It is possible to protect one's offspring against fairies – hanging scissors or shears above cradles might seem a bit dangerous but will do the trick (both because of the iron in the tools and by the shape of the cross formed by the blades), while sprigs of rowan above doorways or windows or even above the crib will also deter the small folk.

Fairies did produce and care for their own offspring as well as stealing human babies, but they sometimes needed human assistance during the birthing process. There are numerous tales of human midwives being pressed into service by the small folk; one Keighley woman was persuaded to accompany a small and wizened old man in order to assist his wife who was in labour. The woman helped the fairy wife to deliver successfully, and she watched the proud father anoint his offspring with some liquid from a phial, to enable the baby to see supernatural beings. Unnoticed, the midwife managed to anoint her own forehead before the fairy took her back home, and from that day she also could see the small folk.

All went well, until one day the woman was at market and noticed the same fairy man as before, only this time he was stealing food from a stall. She approached him and asked how his wife and child were faring, but he reacted with fury and removed her power to see his kind.

Legends of buried treasure, sometimes but not always associated with fairy folk, are often attached to ruins or ancient tunnels and caves. One such is the tale associated with the Iron Age remains at Maiden Castle, in Swaledale. These earthworks are rumoured to be the hiding place of a prodigious hoard of treasure, but when a band of treasure hunters managed to find and unearth the chest on a dark night, a black hen appeared and flapped so violently that

she blew their light out. They relit their lantern and made repeated attempts to open the chest, but to no avail – the hen defended the chest with the furious flapping of her wings. Eventually the men gave up and retreated, but when they returned the next day they were driven back by a violent storm, and were never able to find the chest again.

Finally in this section, there are persistent tales of the fabulous wealth that is said to be hidden in caverns beneath Richmond Castle. A twelve-year-old drummer boy was once persuaded by soldiers to enter a narrow cleft under the castle to search for the gold, since he was the only one of the group small enough to get through the hole the band had found. Once inside the hill he reported that there was a tunnel leading away from the fissure, and his comrades told him to follow it, beating his drum all the while so they could follow his progress on the surface above. The soldiers heard the sound of the drum as he moved away from the hole and were able to follow him, but then suddenly the sounds stopped. The poor boy was never seen again – his comrades assumed that the tunnel had collapsed and buried him – but his drum beat can still sometimes be heard.

HOBS, BOGGARTS AND BARGUESTS

Hobs, boggles or boggarts are often associated with particular Yorkshire places or homesteads, and are distinct from fairies in that they seem to actively seek out people and wish to either help or hinder them. There are numerous examples of hobs who took up residence in farms and houses, and were known to take on work to help their mortal hosts; one such was the hob who lived at Hart Hall on the North York Moors. Like most of his kind he seemed to prefer the hard and menial labour associated with such tasks as threshing, winnowing or sweeping, only asking in return a dish of milk left out in the evening.

These domestic hobs often took the form of small wizened old men, naked except for quantities of shaggy black hair all over their bodies. Householders who happened to catch a glimpse of them sometimes thought to reward them by providing clothes, but the hobs would take enormous umbrage at this, and were even known to abandon their homes after such a gesture. Indeed, the Hart Hall hob did exactly this, leaving in high dudgeon after the master of the house tried to thank him for all his hard work with the gift of a servant's smock.

Some hobs were less benign and helpful, however. These spirits were often held responsible for such domestic disasters as upsetting the milk churn, putting out the fire, knocking items off shelves and tables and so on. Sometimes these mischievous creatures lived outside human habitation and merely dropped in as unwelcome visitors; Obtrusch Rock on Farndale Moor was the home of a hobthrush, a spirit of place living in the wild. An old story attached to this place is that a local farmer was so fed up of mischievous visitations from the hobthrush that he decided to pack up and leave. As he was driving his wagon laden with all his worldly goods away from the farm he passed a neighbour on the road. "I see you're flitting?" asked the man – at which a voice came from one of the milk churns: "Aye, we're flutting." The farmer sighed and turned his wagon round, heading back to the farm and resigned to putting up with the hobthrush's mischief.

There are examples of boggle holes – pot holes or caves occupied by hobs or boggles – throughout Yorkshire, for example at Robin Hood's Bay. There are also some at Runswick Bay on the North Yorkshire coast; the hob that lives in the Hob Holes in these cliffs is known to be able to help humans, if he is so inclined and is asked

Runswick Bay, North Yorkshire – the home of a hob? iStock

politely. A rhyme which has come down the centuries implores him to cure a child of whooping cough: "Hob Hole Hob! Ma bairn's gettin' t'kincough! Tak it off! Tak it off!"

Boggarts were also sometimes known to push or pull unwary travellers to their deaths as they passed by; one such at Hurtle Pot, near Chapel-le-Dale, was thought to grab travellers and haul them down into his hole to drown them in the flooded depths. Mulgrave Woods near Whitby was also the home of a hobthrush, who lived in a cave and seemed to be a jocular sort, fond of creeping up on people and playing practical jokes. (This wood was also supposed to be the home of the fairy Jeanie of Biggersdale – it must have been an unearthly place after dark.)

Barguests or guytreshes are evil spirits which usually take the form of large black spectral animals, often dogs or pigs. They are said to plague travellers on lonely roads (which may have been ancient corpse roads, travelled by funeral processions), and are sometimes thought to be portents of death. Ivelet Bridge, a humpbacked stone packhorse bridge over the River Swale, is said to be haunted by a barguest in the form of a large headless black dog which glides to the edge of the bridge and disappears over the edge.

Similarly, Troller's Gill, a half-mile long and sixty-foot-deep ravine in Wharfedale near Appletreewick, is the home of a particularly fearsome barguest hound with flaming eyes, said by some to be the inspiration for Sir Arthur Conan Doyle's tale of the Hound of the Baskervilles. The hound appears to solitary travellers who dare to enter the gorge at night, sometimes trailing a clanking chain. Troller's Gill is a notoriously sinister and eerie place, and as well as the barguest it is said to be the home of trolls, who inhabit the high rocky walls and whose favourite pastime is dropping stones and rocks on travellers through the gorge who make too much noise.

*High ground on the North York Moors.
The haunt of the Goathland barguest?*
iStock

Yorkshire barguests are sometimes known as guytreshes, padfoots or skrikers, but all have in common that they are usually taken to be a portent of disaster or even death. Sometimes they foretell the death of the person who encounters them, sometimes of someone in his or her family, and sometimes they portend the demise of an important person in the local community. In fact, sometimes the barguest is associated directly with such a person, as with the Goathland barguest which was thought to be the walking spirit of the brutal landlord Julian of Goathland, who died an agonised death as the result of a curse. This barguest terrorised the countryside, afflicting anyone who witnessed it with a mysterious but rapidly fatal malady, until it was trapped in a pit on the advice of a local witch.

An old superstition notes that the people most likely to see barguests are those born under chime hours, or towards the small hours of a Friday night. It is generally held that the best thing to do if encountering a barguest is to ignore it and not interact with it in any way, and evade it if possible. This is not easy, though, since they move fearsomely fast and track their victims closely, and some have even come to their deaths trying to get away – like the young man who thought to lose the Egton barguest by crossing the parish churchyard, but stumbled into an open grave in the darkness and broke his neck.

WITCHES AND
THE DEVIL

Yorkshire was the home of a number of alleged witches over the centuries, with the wild moorlands and mysterious caves and woods providing havens for any misfits who might have wanted to avoid human society. Many lived in towns and villages, however; Susannah Goor, known as the Barrow Witch, lived in Driffield in the late eighteenth and early nineteenth centuries and had a reputation for fortune telling and for being in league with the Devil. Legend has it that she was last seen 'flying ower Driffield Church on a blazin' besom'.

Another Yorkshire witch, named Auld Molly, was accused of stealing milk. The farmer was advised to wait in the field with his cattle overnight, armed with a shotgun and silver bullets (that panacea against all supernatural beasts and beings). However, Molly arrived in the guise of a hare, and proceeded to fix the famer with such a glare from her piercing eyes that he lost his nerve and fled.

It seems hares were a popular shapeshifted form for Yorkshire witches; another witch known as Nanny decided to have some sport with a band of hare coursers. In human form she told them where there was a particularly elusive hare to be found; her condition was that they must not pursue it with black dogs. The coursers went where she directed them; sure enough, there they found a large and swift hare, and they had a great day's sport. Finally the hare led them into the vicinity of Nanny's home, but then the hunters broke their word and released a black dog. The hound chased the hare and wounded it just as it squeezed through a small hole into Nanny's house. The hunters entered the house to find Nanny prostrate on the bed, bleeding from a bite wound to her leg.

Mary Pannell was another Yorkshire witch, a historical figure who is remembered to this day in her local area of Ledston, near Castleford. Mary was a maid at Ledston Hall around 1600, and was a young woman with a reputation as a healer. When the son of the house fell ill his mother sought Mary's aid, and Mary provided a salve. However, the worried mother misunderstood Mary's instructions and gave the salve to the boy to drink, which killed him. Mary was duly accused of witchcraft, tried and found guilty; she was hanged in York, and her body was brought back to Ledston and burned on a hill on the edge of Castleford, which now bears her name.

Like the giants of Yorkshire, the Devil was responsible for many landscape features. He left his hoofprint in a number of places (for example, Scar Top near Huddersfield, Baildon and Rivock Edge in West Yorkshire). He also threw stones, such as the Devil's Arrows at Boroughbridge – an alignment of three huge standing stones, which legend says the Devil threw from nearby Howe Hill in an attempt to destroy the town of Aldborough. As he did so he is said to have proclaimed, "Boroughbridge, keep out o' t'way, for Aldborough I will ding down!" However, they fell short and Aldborough was saved. Likewise, Rudston Monolith, the tallest standing stone in Britain, is situated in a churchyard, and the story is that the Devil threw it in an attempt to destroy the church, missing narrowly.

Legend also states that Filey Brigg, the rocky promontory in Filey Bay, was created by the Devil in an abortive attempt to bridge the

Filey Brigg, North Yorkshire – the Devil's attempt to bridge the North Sea. iStock

North Sea. While he was working on his construction project he accidentally dropped his hammer in the sea; reaching below the water to find it, he grabbed a haddock by mistake. Realising his error he dropped the fish, but not before his thumb and fingers had left striated marks along the fish's flanks, which can be seen to this day.

The Devil is supposed to have first set foot on earth at West Nab, near Meltham, and the Hole of Horcum on the North York Moors, also known as the Devil's Punchbowl, is supposed to be the hole left behind when he scooped up a clod of earth to throw at Scarborough. However, he was distracted by the sun glinting off Lilla Cross, a tenth century Christian monument and boundary marker on Fylingdales Moor, and instead of hurling the earth he dropped it to form Blakey Topping. He is also supposed to have leaped from Roulston Crag to the nearby Hood Hill, accidentally taking with him a massive boulder which had melted and adhered to one of his feet. The rock dropped and still lies on the slopes of Hood Hill, supposedly marked with a hoof-shaped depression.

Kilgram Bridge near Masham stands at the site of a much older ford, but this was prone to flooding, and before the bridge's construction it was a source of much inconvenience to the locals. The Devil offered to build them a bridge, but at the cost that he would claim the soul of the first living thing to cross it. The locals agreed, the bridge was built, and the Devil awaited his payment. However, a cunning shepherd was one step ahead; he swam the river and then whistled for his dog Grim, who obediently trotted across the bridge. Thwarted, the Devil nevertheless claimed his prize and the bridge was named – Kill Grim Bridge.

The petrifying well at Mother Shipton's cave, Knaresborough. iStock

Mother Shipton

The most famous witch and soothsayer in Yorkshire, and perhaps in England, was Mother Shipton. She was born Ursula Southill in a cave near Knaresborough around 1488; her mother Agatha later said that thunder and a smell of sulphur accompanied her birth. Agatha never admitted who Ursula's father was, and handed her over to a local family and entered a convent when her daughter was only two.

Ursula was hounded and tormented as a child because of her fearsome ugliness, and took refuge in the forests near the cave where she was born. She married Toby Shipton around 1521, but the couple were childless and he died a few years later. She kept his name, and became Mother Shipton as she grew older.

She is reputed to have made predictions and prophecies throughout her life, although the first collection was not published in 1641, some eighty years after her death at the venerable age of 73. The most famous of these predictions foretold the end of the world in 1881 (or 1991, depending on which version one reads), but she is also supposed to have predicted the defeat of the Spanish Armada, the Great Fire of London, telephony, powered flight, and many other events around the world. The cave where she was born is open to visitors, containing a petrifying well and claiming to be England's oldest tourist attraction.

Protection Against Witches

Yorkshire folk believed in maleficium – the ill-wishes or curses directed by witches. There were many ways of deflecting or preventing this harm; witch stones or hag stones (pebbles with natural holes in) were kept about the person to serve as talismans, horseshoes were nailed above doors, and rowan wood (also known as wiggin) was used for items such as churn staffs or whip handles, to ward off maleficium directed at the dairy or livestock. Rowan trees were also often planted in and around farmyards and in gardens, to protect the household. Another use of rowan wood was the construction of witchposts – thick wooden posts built into the fabric of houses, often next to fireplaces or hearths, to protect the building and all who lived inside.

Counterspells were sometimes attempted to ward off suspected maleficium from specific witches; these often involved obtaining the blood of the witch concerned, or doing some injury to her, perhaps by pricking her with a pin. Witch bottles were constructed containing hair or nail clippings or even urine of the person afflicted, along with quantities of nails, pins or needles. This mixture was then heated over a fire, which would cause the witch great discomfort and cause her to lift the spell.

Such bottles were sometimes then built into the fabric of buildings, perhaps to protect the inhabitants from similar spells from the same witch. Other items walled up in houses included shoes, cats, or even human remains such as skulls. Burton Agnes Hall in East Yorkshire has its own resident skull – Katherine Griffith died there around 1620, and loved her home so much that she demanded on her deathbed that part of her remain there. She was buried in the graveyard as usual, but her ghost reappeared and caused so much upheaval that she was exhumed and her skull was brought home. Many attempts have been made to remove it, but Katherine always objects so strongly that eventually the owners gave in and walled her up somewhere in the house, where she continues to watch over it to this day.

DRAGONS, WYRMS AND WILD BEASTS

The ancient imagination created monsters aplenty to populate the mysterious landscape, and the wild and rugged parts of Yorkshire have been home to more than their fair share of dragons, serpents and other beasts. Most of these terrors have met their match in local heroes, but the day does not always end well for the would-be dragon-slayers, some of whom gave their lives to save the local population from the beasts' depredations.

The road from Hovingham to Malton along the northern line of the Howardian Hills does not pass through the village of Slingsby, instead veering to the south. The story is that there was once a terrible serpent who lived in a deep hole near the village and preyed on travellers, necessitating a change to the route of the road to avoid the creature's lair. However, a heroic local landowner named Sir William Wyvill tired of this inconvenience, and with the help of his dog he slew the monster. However, both man and dog died themselves in the battle, and an unnamed tomb in Slingsby Church is said to commemorate them.

There was also a dragon at Wharncliffe Side, this time slain by a colourful hero known as More of More Hall. His tale is commemorated in a ribald and entertaining popular operetta of the eighteenth century, *The Dragon of Wantley*, recounting how More agreed to rid the locals of the beast but demanded his payment up front, in the shape of a village maiden to tend him. Once his new servant was in place he got himself rigged out in an outlandish suit of armour complete with spikes, hid in a well, punched the dragon in the face when it came to drink, and eventually killed it by kicking it up the fundament with his spiked boot.

Many serpents and dragons have associations with landscape features such earthworks, barrows, hills, caves and so on. Most were also associated with nearby towns or settlements, and the battles to defeat them are often commemorated in the landscape. The Handale Serpent was a fiery creature, which preyed on women until it was slain by a youth called Scaw. Likewise, the Nunnington Worm was killed by a local knight named Sir Peter Loschy, but not easily. The beast healed itself after each blow, and although Sir Peter fought bravely he could make no headway — until, that is, he hacked off a piece of the beast and his dog carried it away and buried it. The pair, man and dog, repeated this until the dragon grew weak and eventually died. Today, Scaw Wood near Handale and Loschy Hill near Nunnington are examples of dragon-slayers given permanent memorials in the landscape.

A Whitby legend tells that the redoubtable Abbess Hild, the founder and ruler of Whitby Abbey in the seventh century, rid the entirety of Eskdale of serpents by driving them over the cliff into the sea at the mouth of the Esk river at Whitby. This is evidenced by the coiled stones commonly to be found on the beach at Whitby (more usually known these days as ammonites).

As well as being the remains of the Devil's attempt to bridge the North Sea, Filey Brigg, the rocky promontory in Filey Bay, is also said to be the body of a slain dragon. The worm lived in a ravine near Filey, into which fell a local tailor named Billy. The dragon was about to eat him, but then a piece of his wife's parkin fell out of his pocket and the dragon ate that instead. The creature liked the cake so much that he sent Billy home to his wife to fetch more.

The cliffs at Whitby. iStock

However, Billy's wife didn't believe his tale, and insisted on taking the parkin herself. She must have been a little anxious, however, for she fortified her courage with a drink or two on the way, and by the time she got to the ravine she was unsteady on her feet and fell in herself. The dragon ate her parkin, and then ate her.

The cake is notoriously sticky, though, and a morsel of it lodged in the dragon's teeth. He went down to the sea to wash it out, whereupon a band of locals assembled with pitchforks and sledgehammers to prevent it returning to shore. The creature drowned in Filey Bay, and its bones now form the rocky promontory of the Brigg.

The Bradford Boar? iStock

Other creatures were not supernatural in origin, however – merely large and ferocious. The Bradford Boar lived in Cliffe Wood, terrorising the inhabitants of the then-small settlement of Bradford and drinking from the well which was the village's sole source of water. The villagers were too scared to visit the well in case they encountered the beast, and this dire situation soon reached the ears of the local lord of the manor.

He decided that something must be done, so he offered a substantial reward in land and money to anyone who could kill the boar – but in order to claim the prize they must bring the creature's head as proof. One wily huntsman lay in wait for the beast near the well, and when it came to drink he sprang up and killed it with his bow and arrows and a sturdy spear.

However, when the beast lay dead the huntsman realised that it was of such prodigious size that he stood no chance of being able to carry its head back to the lord of the manor. Being a crafty sort, he decided to cut out its tongue as evidence, and having done so he set off back to claim his reward.

Shortly afterwards a second huntsman came across the corpse, and saw an opportunity to benefit from someone else's error. He cut off the boar's head with his sword, and being bigger and stronger than the first huntsman, and also knowing a shortcut back to the manor house, he hefted the head all the way back and arrived first.

The lord of the manor was duly impressed by the size and ferocity of the boar, even in death, and was just about to hand over the reward when he noticed that the creature's tongue was missing. The opportunist huntsman had no explanation for this, at which point the first hunter arrived and produced the tongue, denouncing his rival. The lord of the manor immediately saw what had happened and gave the prize to the rightful winner – a parcel of land which to this day is known as Hunt Yard.

A similar tale is told of the Felon Sow of Rokeby which terrorised part of the North Riding, living wild in the woods and stalking the riverbanks of the River Greta. The lord of Rokeby tired of this and offered the sow to the Greyfriars of Richmond, on the condition that they could catch her. A Friar named Middleton was deputed to achieve this and set off into the woods accompanied by two local men as an escort, confident of returning with the sow safely dead and strung up between them.

Sure enough, they soon trapped the sow in an old lime kiln, and attempted to tie her up. However, the sow had other ideas and burst out of her prison and set upon her captors, routing the escort and forcing the poor Friar to climb a tree to escape.

Eventually Friar Middleton was able to make his way down the tree and back to the village, where he hired two men at arms. He extracted from them a solemn vow that they would 'bide and fight', and in return the other Greyfriars agreed to say masses for their souls if they should all die. Then they all set off back to the woods.

Being stronger and more experienced than the villagers, the men at arms soon defeated the sow, and she was brought to the Greyfriars' abbey where she was regarded as a great prize. This is a rare folk tale which has a happy outcome for everyone (except for the sow) – the lord is rid of the menace to his lands, the Greyfriars win their prize, and even the men at arms win gratitude and the promise of divine intercession. There is even an aspect of poking fun at the Church, with the image of Friar Middleton scrambling up a tree in his grey robes to avoid the raging sow!

WATER LORE

The powerful and liminal nature of water has caused the accumulation of many legends and myths associated with rivers, lakes, wells and springs. The Ebbing and Flowing Well, near Giggleswick, is an example of a good story attaching itself to a natural but mysterious phenomenon. This curiosity is so called because of its habit of rapidly draining and then refilling itself, with no apparent warning or reason. This is now a less common occurrence than it used to be, but it does still happen from time to time, with the well even occasionally overflowing and running over the nearby busy road.

Local folklore states that the well's odd behaviour is because a nymph was being pursued by an amorous satyr and called on the gods for help. They took pity on her and transformed her into a spring of water, which ebbs and flows with her sighs and panting breaths. Good fortune will also come to anyone who sees the rare 'silver thread' or spiral of trapped air as the well empties.

The well has a link with John 'Swift Nick' Nevison, who is thought to have encountered a wise woman who lived nearby and who gave him magical aid. He went on to evade capture after his horse drank from the well and was granted strength to leap great distances. There are a number of scars, cuttings, chasms or gullies throughout Yorkshire that are still known as still known as Nevison's Leap; one such nearby is a deep cutting through the rock between Pontefract and Ferrybridge, across which Nevison's horse is said to have leaped to throw off pursuers.

A spring, North Yorkshire. iStock

Similarly, Walton Well near Wakefield also had a connection with Swift Nick; he was supposedly surprised while resting there and fled, giving rise to the term 'Walton calf' to refer to a faint-hearted or cowardly man. (It is certain that Nevison would have had to stop regularly to allow his horse to drink during his notorious dash from Rochester to York in 1676, so perhaps that explains the frequency with which his name is associated with wells and springs in the region.) The waters of Walton Well were also supposed to have healing properties for those afflicted by eye diseases, and nearby trees were once festooned with clooties or rags which were tied in there as votive offerings.

Other wells were thought to be the homes of fairies, who would grant wishes or visions in exchange for the offering of a crooked pin thrown into the waters. It was thought that the fairies wanted the pins to use as arrowheads, but were unable to obtain iron in any other way and were therefore forced into this unwilling trade.

Of course, water in past ages was not the clean, sterilised resource we have access to today. Water sources such as rivers, streams and springs easily became contaminated, and in Yorkshire it was believed that anyone who became ill after drinking dirty water had ingested a creature known as a 'watter wolf'. This being would take up residence in their digestive tract and would cause them to sicken and die unless it was somehow expelled or killed by the use of charms or folk remedies.

Some Yorkshire rivers were home to kelpies or water horses. The River Ure, near Middleham in Wensleydale, is said to be the haunt of one such, which gallops through waterside meadows in the evenings and is thought to claim at least one human victim a year. The notoriously treacherous Bolton Strid, on the River Wharfe, is the home of another, appearing out of the churning waters to presage a death in the river. One such was that of young William FitzDuncan, also known as the Boy of Egremont – he was the only male heir to the Barony of Copeland in Cumbria, but around 1160 he attempted to leap the Strid during a hunting expedition, and was drowned when his hound balked at the jump, yanking back on its leash and caused the Boy to lose his footing and plunge into the churning waters. It is said the white horse of the Strid appeared before the tragic accident, but the Boy took no heed, and the male line of Copeland died out as a result.

Semer Water, the largest natural lake in North Yorkshire, is said to have once been the site of a wealthy and prosperous town. An old vagrant visited and sought shelter and food from its inhabitants, but the proud and selfish townsfolk turned him away at every door. Finally giving up, the old man left the town and called instead at a small and poor homestead on the slopes above the town, where a shepherd and his wife insisted that he share their food and their home overnight. In the morning, as he left the old man paused and stood looking down at the town in the valley below him. Raising his arms, he called on the waters to rise and swallow the

The River Wharfe. iStock

arrogant settlement, and sure enough a deluge drowned the town but stopped short of the house where he had been given bed and board.

A similar tale is told of Gormire, although this inundation was said to be the result of an earthquake rather than a judgement on the townsfolk. When the waters are clear it may sometimes be possible to see the remains of buildings far below the surface of the water.

HEROES AND VILLAINS

There are some heroes of myth and legend who permeate the national consciousness. Everyone knows their name and can recount at least one or two of their exploits; everyone knows where they lived and who their allies and enemies were. However, each area of the country also has its own local heroes, whose deeds are much more closely tied to the immediate area and who may be remembered in folk customs or rituals.

Of course, sometimes these two types overlap, with local customs and stories associated with national figures. In this section you will meet some of the heroes and villains who are known and remembered in Yorkshire.

Robin Hood

Although Robin Hood is more often associated in the popular imagination with Nottinghamshire and Sherwood Forest, the area of southern Yorkshire known as Barnsdale, near Pontefract, also features in many tales related to the famous outlaw; indeed, some suspect that the legend was born there, probably around the fourteenth century, and migrated to other parts of the country in

Scene from Robin Hood of Barnsdale.
iStock

later years. The hero is said to have been born on a farm at Loxley, near Sheffield, but was forced to flee and become an outlaw when he killed his father with a scythe.

There are many tales of Robin Hood's antics and escapades which are said to have taken place in Yorkshire – for example, the friar who was known in later tales as Tuck is said to have lived close to Fountains Abbey, near Ripon, and joined Robin's band when he bested the famous outlaw in a battle of brawn and wits. Another tale relates how Robin retired from outlawry to the coast near Scarborough, where he took up fishing. Being inexperienced, he was mocked by his crewmates until a French warship hove into view and threatened their craft and its crew with capture and slavery. Robin saved his shipmates by breaking out his bow and shooting many of the French crew, eventually boarding the vessel and seizing a sizable amount of gold as a prize. True to his characteristic generosity, he tried to share the treasure with his friends, but they insisted he had won it singlehanded and should keep it all.

Robin Hood's Well at Skellow is easily visible from the Great North Road (once the Roman route known as Watling Street, now the A1, and still the main trunk road running north to south up the spine of Britain). The modern stone well structure was designed by Vanbrugh and was moved to its present location when the A1 was widened, but it used to mark the location nearby where Robin Hood and his men are said to have dressed as shepherds and waylaid the Bishop of Hereford and his retinue, sharing a meal of venison with them and then forcing them to pay handsomely for the meal.

Of course, the town of Robin Hood's Bay on the North Yorkshire coast owes its name to the famous outlaw; the story here is that the king sent soldiers from London to deal with the notorious band,

and Robin and his men went into hiding in the wilds of the North York Moors. However, Robin kept a boat moored in a coastal inlet in case he should need to escape by sea, and often took it out fishing while he was in the area. The inlet took his name, and the town grew up in that location.

Perhaps the most poignant episode in Robin Hood's story – his death – is also said to have taken place in Yorkshire. In age and infirmity Robin sought help from his aunt, the Prioress of Kirklees Abbey, near Brighouse, travelling there with the faithful Little John. Entering the Abbey alone, Robin asked the Prioress to bleed him, a common treatment in the Middle Ages, but instead she opened his vein and then left him alone in a locked chamber to bleed to death – perhaps in reprisal for all his robberies from the Church over the years. Realising what had happened, Robin blew his hunting horn and summoned Little John from the surrounding forest. John brought Robin's bow, and with his last strength Robin shot an arrow into the trees. An ancient stone monument on land once owned by Kirklees Abbey is said to mark the spot where the arrow fell, and where Robin is buried with his sword, bow and arrows.

Robin Hood's Bay, where the famous outlaw kept a fishing boat. iStock

John (Swift Nick) Nevison

John Nevison was a notorious highwayman, active in the century before the more famous Dick Turpin. Nevison was probably born at Wortley, between Barnsley and Sheffield, around 1639. Evidence suggests he ran away from home in his early teens and spent time in London and then in the Duke of York's army in Holland, taking part in the Battle of Dunkirk against the Spanish in 1658.

After his discharge he returned to Britain, but struggled to settle into civilian life and eventually became a highwayman, as many ex-soldiers did. Based around Newark, he had a reputation as a gentleman rogue, never using violence against his victims. Along with a small band of associates he targeted travellers along the Great North Road, using safe houses at Tuxford in Nottinghamshire and Wentbridge, near Pontefract.

He earned his soubriquet of Swift Nick because of a famous ride from Rochester to York in the summer of 1676. He robbed a traveller in the early morning at Gad's Hill, near Rochester in

York — the destination for Swift Nick's famous ride, and the place of his execution. iStock

Kent, but was recognised. Escaping the hue and cry, he crossed the Thames and proceeded to gallop two hundred miles north to York, resting his bay mare at intervals before pushing on. Arriving in York near sunset, he stabled his weary mount, freshened himself and then strolled to a bowling green where he made a point of talking to the Lord Mayor of the city, marking the time as eight o'clock in the course of the conversation.

He was later arrested and brought to trial for the robbery, but built his defence on the argument that he could not have committed the crime since he had been in York that evening and no one could possibly have made that journey in a single day. He called the Lord Mayor as his alibi and was duly acquitted, emerging from the affair a folk hero and earning the attention and admiration of King Charles II, who gave him the title Swift Nick.

He went on to be arrested many more times – once he was sentenced to deportation to Tangiers but jumped ship and returned to robbery, and on another occasion he avoided trial by getting an accomplice to pronounce him dead of the plague before making his escape. He was finally taken in 1684 when the landlady of the Magpie Inn in Sandal, near Wakefield, tipped off bounty hunters. He was tried for the final time and hanged at the Knavesmire in York in May 1684, and is buried in an unmarked grave in the churchyard of St Mary's in the city (now an arts venue).

King Arthur

There are not many Arthurian connections in Yorkshire (it being outside his traditional stamping ground of Wessex), but one story holds that he sleeps with a dozen of his knights in a chamber below Richmond Castle in North Yorkshire. A local man named Potter

Thompson is said to have taken a long walk on day to escape his harridan of a wife, and stumbled across a fissure in the rocks below the castle. Exploring the cavern, Potter followed a passageway to reach a lit chamber where Arthur was arrayed on a stone table in armour and crown, with his knights slumbering around him and a horn and sword hung on the rocky wall nearby. Potter grasped and began to draw the sword, but as he did so the knights began to stir, whereupon he lost his nerve and fled.

A voice pursued him, stating that if he had blown the horn or drawn the sword he would have become the luckiest man alive. Recovering his courage some time later he tried to go back, but he could never locate the cavern again.

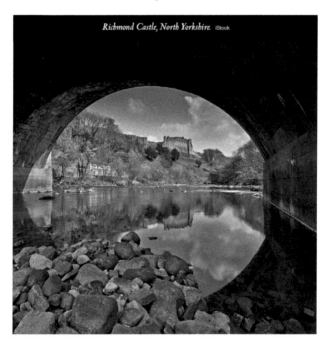

Richmond Castle, North Yorkshire. iStock

The Burning of Bartle

One of the oddest Yorkshire heroes (or villains – no one seems quite sure) is Owd Bartle. He is commemorated yearly in the village of West Witton, in Wensleydale, with a ceremonial burning of his effigy on the Saturday nearest to August 24 (St Bartholomew's Day). Coincidentally (or perhaps not), St Bartholomew is the patron saint of the parish church.

The straw effigy of Bartle is paraded around the village with much repetition of the following doggerel rhyme:

On Penhill Crags he tore his rags;
Hunter's Thorn he blew his horn;
Cappelbank Stee happened a misfortune and broke his knee;
Grassgill Beck he broke his neck;
Wadhams End he couldn't fend;
Grassgill End we'll mak' his end.
Shout, lads, shout!

His bearers stop at various hostelries for refreshment before arriving at a spot by a wall at Grassgill End, where he is set alight amid much singing and carousing.

There are many different theories as to origin of the tradition. Some hold that Bartle was a local man who stole his neighbours' sheep. He was discovered, tried at the village court and an example made of him by ritual burning. This seems harsh, but livestock theft would have been a serious matter in a farming community.

However, others identify Bartle with Bartholomew, the saint of the local church, and interpret the procession around the village as a survival of the pre-Reformation custom of parading the saint's icon — or even of the villagers' attempts to hide his effigy or relics during the Reformation itself. Still others suggest that the tradition is a folk memory of a much older pagan ritual, possibly connected with the harvest. Whether any of these theories approach the truth may never be known, but the custom is certainly alive and well in West Witton, with Bartle's fiery demise now part of a weekend of carnival festivities.

Black sheep near West Witton — perhaps descended from Owd Bartle's booty. iStock

SUPERSTITIONS AND OMENS

The uncertainty and precariousness of life in bygone centuries meant that signs, symbols and superstitions were treated with great importance. Life was ruled by observations and omens, and the closeness of our rural ancestors' relationship with the natural world around them meant that many of these proverbs referred to the behaviour of plants, animals and even the weather – and some were in rhyming form, perhaps to aid the memory. For example:

Hawthorn bloom and elder flowers
Will fill a house with evil powers

When old cats play, rain is on the way

If there's ice in November to hold a duck,
There will be a winter of slush and muck

If the moon on a Saturday be new or full,
There always was rain and there always will.

Onion skins very thin: a mild winter coming in.
Onion skins thick and tough: coming winter wild and rough.

If spiders are many and spinning their webs, the weather will soon be very dry.

When pine cones open on the trees, the weather is set fine.

Oak before ash – we're in for a splash;
Ash before oak – we're in for a soak.

Household activities were set about with superstitions of all kinds. A hat on a bed brought bad luck, while a candle flickering or burning with a blue flame indicated the presence of a spirit in the room. Other proverbs and sayings related to commerce or education (although they may not be taken as the truth nowadays!). For example:

He that buys land buys many stones,
He that buys flesh buys many bones,
He that buys eggs buys many shells,
But he that buys good ale buys nothing else.

A cow, a sow and a woman – you can learn them nothing,
A dog, a horse and a man – you can learn them anything.

An old Yorkshire superstition claims that no one should poke the fire who has not known the householder for at least seven years. Meanwhile, harvesting of certain crops was thought to be related to the phase of the moon, as shown in this rhyme:

When the moon is at the full,
Mushrooms you may freely pull;
But when the moon is on the wane,
Wait 'ere you think to pluck again.'

Good Luck, Bad Luck

According to our rural ancestors, if you want to avoid bad luck you should avoid doing the following:

Walking under a ladder

Putting shoes or boots on the table

Shaking hands across the dinner table

Spilling salt on the table

Singing at the table

Sleeping on the table

Placing your knife and fork crossways on your plate

Turning your bed on a Sunday

Brushing the dust out of the front door

Giving gloves as a present

Cutting your fingernails on a Monday, Friday or Sunday

Opening an umbrella in the house

Bringing thyme into the house

Carrying anything on your shoulder in the house

Entering a house for the first time through the back door

Throwing dead flowers onto the fire

Cutting down a flowering tree

Turning back after beginning a journey

Doing anything on Friday 13th

Nailing up a horseshoe with the points down (all the luck will drain out)

Killing a sparrow (they carry the souls of the dead)

Breaking a mirror

Likewise, to ensure good luck you should:

Carry a piece of coal in your pocket

Carry a piece of iron with a hole in it

Carry a rabbit's foot

Keep a lock of hair from a baby's first haircut

Burn your tea leaves

Salute a solitary magpie

Wish on a falling star

Bow nine times to the new moon

Cut your fingernails on a Thursday

Put on your left sock or stocking first when getting dressed

Pick up a pin if you see one

Pick up a white stone, spit on it and throw it over your head

Take a snail by its horns and throw it backwards over your shoulder

Throw a pinch of salt over your left shoulder

Begin a journey with your right foot first

Look for a four-leaved clover

Look for a double-leaved sprig of ash

Let a black cat cross your path

Nail up a horseshoe with the points upwards (to keep the luck intact)

Cross your fingers if you accidentally do anything unlucky

Catch a falling leaf — the more you catch, the more good luck you will have

The Journey Through Life

Life was more precarious in the past. A lack of understanding as to what caused diseases or the knowledge of how to cure them meant mortality rates were high, especially among children. For the same reason, accidents involving injury were also far more serious. Wars were more frequent, too.

The perilous journey through life had important stages which were celebrated with ritual and accompanied by superstition. There were several strange beliefs regarding the beginning of life. It was said that a child born at midnight would have second sight, and that a 'footling' – that is, a baby born feet first — would have magical powers. Efforts were made to preserve the caul surrounding the child at birth because it was thought to be possessed with sympathetic magic. Kept safe, it would prevent the person it belonged to from suffering death by drowning. There are records from well into the twentieth century of sailors buying cauls in the belief they would keep them safe.

As soon as a woman went into labour, a party called a Merry Meet would be held at her house. The prospective father would entertain family and neighbours, and a 'groaning cheese' and a 'groaning cake' would be carefully cut into exactly the right number of pieces to serve to the guests. Unfortunately, of course, the woman giving birth was unable to enjoy the festivities herself.

With infant mortality so high, it was considered essential to christen a newborn baby as soon as possible. An unbaptised child would not go to heaven, but some thought they might become fairies instead. If the baptism was performed at home the water used to christen the child was often thrown into the fire, to ensure it remained pure and no evil influence could pollute it. While the child was still unbaptised it was customary to make them a gift of an egg (symbolising new life), some salt and, unsafe though it may seem, a box of matches. Salt and fire were considered sure charms against the attentions of evil spirits.

Even after baptism the infant might be at risk from fairies, who were thought to cast acquisitive eyes at human children. To ward them off, parents might hang a pair of scissors or tongs over the crib, which would dangle in the form of a cross. The cross shape and the iron in the scissors were sure protection against the little people.

At one time new mothers genuinely feared their children might be stolen by fairies unless they protected them with certain charms before they were baptised.

Some mothers would bite their children's fingernails short rather than cutting them. It was believed that if they cut the fingernails, the child would grow up to be a thief. It was also said that a new baby must always be carried upstairs before it goes down, otherwise it would not rise in life. If there were no stairs in the house, the midwife would climb onto a chair with it.

In young adulthood, there were also some interesting customs surrounding courtship. We tend to assume morals were more conservative in the past, so it may be a surprise to learn that courting couples were often allowed to sleep together undisturbed. However, this was only with the proviso that the young man kept his clothes on (minus his coat and boots). A variant custom called 'bundling' allowed the couple to share a bed with a bolster between them. Such would have been the disgrace if the young couple abused this trust that few did. Mind you, engagements tended to be shorter in those days.

A young woman hoping to marry into a farming family was often called upon to prove her strength by lifting with one arm the heavy lid of the parish chest in the church. The parish chest contained charitable donations and other valuables and was usually made of thick oak, bound with stout iron. To lift it with one arm could be quite a feat.

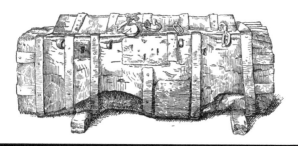

An example of a parish chest, an ancient and massive casket sometimes carved out of one solid piece of oak. Lifting its heavy lid with one arm would be hard work for most men, let alone the young women who were expected to do it.

As to the wedding day itself, there was an ancient custom in which the friends of the groom would call at the bride's house with a view to 'abducting' her. Her duty was to hide, so as to avoid this indignity, or – better still – to sneak to the church before they caught her. This was a remnant of a much older custom in which young men would prove their worth by stealing the girl they fancied from under her parents' roof. In more civilised times, no abduction or manhandling of the bride actually took place and the whole thing was done in fun.

A rather unkind superstition related to weddings was that if a woman served as a bridesmaid three times, she would never be married herself. Likewise, a man who acted as best man three times would never wed. But there are even stranger ones; for example, if a young woman puts on a man's hat or a young man puts on a woman's hat, they will have to wait three years before they can get married. If a young person cuts bread obliquely or in uneven slices they will never be married, they may have to wait seven years, or else they will end up with an objectionable mother-in-law. If a girl touches the foot of another girl with a broom while sweeping, she will rob that girl of her future husband. Finally, when the bride enters the church, she must never look behind her or she will end up regretting the marriage.

There are equally strange superstitions regarding the final great change in a person's life – death. Dogs howling or owls screeching might be taken as omens of a coming death. Clocks suddenly stopping or chiming thirteen were a bad sign, as were a robin tapping at the window pane, a crow getting into the house or an owl settling on the roof. Mysterious noises such as knocks and raps in a house where someone lay ill were also ominous. Carpenters sometimes claimed they heard sounds in their workshops at night resembling those of a coffin being made. They knew then that one would soon be ordered.

When the last moment seemed to be nigh, people were sometimes 'helped to die' by those looking after them. All the doors and windows in the house were opened wide to allow the soul to escape. At the same time, knots were untied, mirrors covered and the fire – the 'soul of the house' – was put out. 'Passing bells' were traditionally rung nine times to announce a death, but their original purpose was to scare away any evil spirits seeking to claim the soul of the departed. A plate of salt, a substance long believed to ward off evil, was placed on the body. No corpse was left with its eyes open, for it was said that it would be looking for the next person to die.

After a death, the household would 'keep watch' for at least one night while the corpse lay in the house because it was thought that the soul of the departed might return. Sometimes the assembly would chant 'It is for the last time, it is the last night', in order to remind the spirit that it had to pass on. If the master of the house died it was considered important to inform the bees in the hive of the fact, otherwise they would all fly away. Any significant tree or bush, even household plants, were at one time draped with black crêpe after a death, because it was feared that otherwise they would wither away.

When the corpse was conveyed to its burial place it had to be taken to its grave in the same direction as the sun passes through the sky – that is, 'deosil' or clockwise. To take it in the opposite direction, 'widdershins' or anti-clockwise, would make the soul vulnerable to malign forces. There was a prejudice about being the first person buried in a new graveyard, because it was said that the Devil had the right to claim the first corpse. Another superstition suggested that the spirit of the most recent person to be buried haunted a graveyard, watching over it until another burial took place.

A decidedly primitive custom, which had all but died out by the end of the nineteenth century, was that of the 'sin-eater'. The sin-eater was usually a poor member of the parish who was prepared, for a small fee and a meal, to spiritually take on the sins of a person who had just died. This would be achieved by offering them specially baked cakes, or bread on a dish of salt, the eating of which meant that he would absorb the sins. The food might even be offered over the coffin of the dead person; at any rate, the meal would always be eaten in the graveyard. This belief seems to hark back to the time when our most distant ancestors believed they could take on the power and attributes of a deceased person by devouring their body. The sin-eater was therefore a kind of spiritual cannibal.

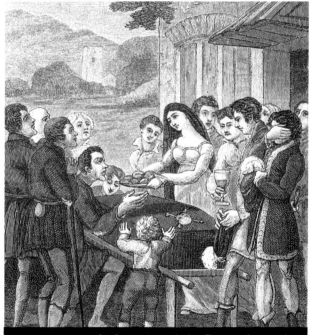

A poor person is offered food over a coffin so that he will eat away the sins of the recently deceased.

The Wheel of the Year

The rural calendar was marked by a series of high days and festivals intended to mark crucial times for sowing, reaping and other agricultural activities. These were often of great antiquity, pre-dating the Christian era. Many were adopted by the Church, although rededicated and renamed, and have therefore been preserved down the years.

The Celtic New Year was marked on 1 November, when winter began. The coming dark days were defied with a great celebratory feast called Samhain. Bonfires were lit, animals were mated for the following spring, and any surplus beasts were slaughtered to fatten everyone up in advance of the approaching cold. Guy Fawkes Night is a survival of the Samhain bonfire festival, merely put back a few days and given a political context which would have meant nothing to our pagan ancestors.

As a transient period between the old year and the new, Samhain was considered a time when spirits from the underworld could revisit the earth. It was a time of ghosts and witches. This ancient belief is recalled in our modern-day Hallowe'en traditions. The Church diffused the apparent menace in this festival by dedicating 1 November to all the saints in heaven. Hallows is an archaic word for saints, and Hallowe'en is a contraction of All Hallows Eve – that is, the night before All Hallows or All Saints Day.

In certain parts of Yorkshire Hallowe'en was known as Nutty Crack Night. The tradition associated with this was for a courting couple to throw two nuts in the fire. If they burned together, this was a prediction of married bliss. If they cracked and flew apart, this was considered a sure sign that the relationship would not last.

It was formerly the custom around this time to go Soul Caking, roaming the parish in request of small gifts of money and specially baked dainties called soul cakes. Yorkshire folk knew the 1 and 2 November as Cakin' Neet and All Souls' Day. Square cakes or loaves containing dried fruit, known in Yorkshire as Saumas Loaves, were distributed to callers on the eve before All Souls' Day. Guisers or mummers also put on plays and entertainments, usually disguised or with their faces blackened.

The next great festival in the Celtic calendar was Imbolc, on 1 February. This marked the beginning of the lambing season and is echoed in the Christian Feast of the Purification of the Virgin Mary, or Candlemas, celebrated the following day. Candlemas was dedicated to new mothers and childbirth.

The start of summer was celebrated on 1 May, in the Celtic festival called Beltane. Given over to fertility and the reawakening of the earth, this was a free-for-all party, with singing, dancing, the lighting of more bonfires and a certain amount of licence. May Day continued the tradition in a diluted form. Dancing round the maypole, a pretty ritual, probably replaced a more ribald ceremony.

The last of the big four Celtic festivals took place on 1 August and was called Lugnasadh. This was the harvest festival, when the grain would be gathered in. The Christianised Saxons knew it as *hlaf-maesse*, meaning 'loaf-mass', which later became corrupted to Lammas or Lammastide. The first loaves of bread made from the harvested grain were dedicated to God in a more general Festival of the First Fruits.

The charming custom of dancing round the maypole had its origin in a pagan fertility festival. iStock

In between these four seasonal festivals were many others, some pagan and some of Christian origin, and others, like Easter and Christmas, a blend of the two. Lupercalia, the Roman celebration of youth, took place in the middle of February. In the warmer climes of the east it served as something of a harbinger of spring in which young people were encouraged to choose lovers. It had a reputation for excess that was thoroughly defused by the adoption in its place of the feast honouring the martyrdom of St Valentine, which took place on 14 February. Valentine was a gentleman committed to chastity, and it seems his association with romantic love was merely a matter of convenience. Nonetheless, St Valentine's Day remains one of the most popular traditions in the modern calendar, and people have been exchanging love tokens on this day for centuries.

The old Yorkshire tradition of barring out took place on Shrove Tuesday, at the start of Lent. School children would lock their schoolmaster outside until he granted them a holiday on that day (this sometimes also took place on Guy Fawkes Night, when the traditional parkins were eaten in celebration). Traditionally the Friday after Shrove Tuesday was known in Yorkshire as Kissin' Day, when boys had the right to kiss any girl they choose (but only once).

The fifth Sunday in Lent (Passion Sunday, a week before Palm Sunday and a fortnight before Easter) is known in Yorkshire coastal towns as Carlin Sunday. Traditionally on this day, carlin peas (a hard brown heritage variety) are cooked and seasoned with pepper before being eaten. This custom is said to relate to a ship which wrecked near Filey Brigg and lost its cargo of peas, which washed up on the nearby beaches and were scavenged and consumed by the locals.

Although Easter honours the crucifixion and resurrection of Christ, there are many secular traditions attached to it which date from pre-Christian times. It's likely that the name Easter has been borrowed from a pagan goddess of the spring, Eostre. The Easter Bunny may well be a descendant of the hare, an animal associated with the spring and fertility and sacred to the Celts.

Eggs are a natural symbol of rebirth and were equally appropriate for both the Resurrection and for spring, the season in which Easter falls. It was once a common pastime on Easter Day for people to roll gaily coloured hard-boiled eggs down hillsides in a jovial race. This was called 'pace-egging', and it was once common in Yorkshire. It has been suggested that the rolling eggs represented the life-giving sun's passage through the sky, but it was also widely believed that if one's egg reached the bottom of the hill unscathed, good luck would surely follow.

Hard-boiled 'pace eggs', brightly coloured with vegetable dyes, were rolled down hills in an old Easter custom. iStock

'Lifting' was a widespread and peculiar custom, which was once carried out at Easter but has now died out. It took place on Easter Monday and Tuesday. A chair would be garlanded with flowers and people would take it in turns to sit in it while their fellows raised them into the air. It was common for men to lift women on Easter Monday and the other way round on Easter Tuesday. A pleasant performance in the villages, it could be a rowdy affair in towns, where strangers were sometimes bundled into the chair and forced to pay a fee in order to be let down again.

Other traditions relating to Easter are unarguably Christian, however. On Good Friday, the day of Christ's Crucifixion, we still eat hot cross buns. At one time it was common for all loaves to be marked with a cross. Despite its name, Good Friday's association made it an unlucky day in the minds of our ancestors. It has become a bank holiday because those engaged in dangerous occupations, such as mining and fishing, refused to work on that day. Blacksmiths and those in the building trades would often down tools too, because it was considered poor taste to handle nails on that day.

The following two days were quite different in character. Easter Sunday was always given over to worship and Monday was a holiday given over to leisure and sports. Easter Monday was known in parts of Yorkshire as Leggin' Day, when children would lie in wait to leg each other (trip each other up). Some believed that the sun danced on Easter Day in joyous memory of the resurrection, and it was formerly a custom to rise before dawn in the hope of seeing this phenomenon. It was also traditional to wear new clothes on Easter Day, or at least one item that had never been worn before.

The strange custom of lifting was popular on Easter Monday and the following Tuesday but has now completely died out.

Beating the bounds was another ritual commonly carried out at this time of the year, usually on Ascension Day (5 May). In the days before maps were freely available, it was important to clearly define parish boundaries and to ensure that nothing had occurred to alter them. Beating the bounds was sometimes taken rather too literally, however. The villagers, accompanied by a clergyman, would take the young boys of the parish on a tour of the landmarks on its boundary. At each one they would pause and the boys would be whipped to make sure they remembered them. The clergyman would often bless the landmarks, too, especially wells.

In Whitby, Ascension Eve is marked by the construction of the Whitby Penny Hedge. This is a short length of fencing constructed of hazel and willow, erected on the town's foreshore in the morning. Traditionally the hedge must be constructed using only a penny knife, and it must be strong enough to withstand three tides. The story goes that the annual construction of this hedge was laid on the people of the town as a penance for the unlawful killing of a local hermit, who gave shelter to a boar that was being hunted by a group of the town's men.

The day before the feast of St John the Baptist, or St John's Eve, falls on 23 June. It was also known as Midsummer Eve, even though the summer solstice – the longest day of the year – falls a couple of days before. Once again, this important stage in the year was celebrated with the lighting of bonfires. There were also numerous customs and celebrations associated with the bringing in of the harvest in the autumn, and traditional fairs and sales were held at Michaelmas, on 29 September.

The final great festival of the winter was, of course, Christmas. There is in fact no biblical reference to the date of Christ's birthday, and 25 December was chosen because it coincided with ancient pagan rituals associated with the winter solstice, the shortest day of the year, and with the birth dates of rival gods such as Mithras – 25 December became the Festival of the Unconquered Sun during the reign of the Roman Emperor Aurelius. It made sense for the early Christians to adopt a day already given over to celebration, especially one relating to the sense of hope engendered by the start of longer days and shorter nights.

Many of the old traditional customs associated with Christmas are of pre-Christian origin. Prince Albert, Queen Victoria's husband, is famously credited with bringing the custom of decorating a fir tree to Britain from his native Germany. In fact, there are records of an evergreen tree lit with candles being set up in a London street as long ago as the fifteenth century. This seems to have been a Norse tradition, as was the selecting of a Yule log, although the word 'Yule' is Anglo-Saxon in origin.

The lighting of fires was a central element to the ancient Celtic celebrations. Fire gave warmth and light, allowed food to be cooked and represented that great life-bringer, the sun. Fire therefore brought luck and scared away the powers of darkness. The Yule log would be selected with great ceremony and celebration, in much the way we would choose a Christmas tree today. The larger the fireplace, the larger the log chosen to fill it. Lighting the log became traditional on Christmas Eve, ideally from a saved fragment from the previous year, and if it was big enough, it might bring warmth throughout Christmas Day and beyond.

Holly became associated with Christmas because it is an evergreen, and mistletoe simply because it was the plant most sacred to our Celtic ancestors. According to a Roman historian, the druids would only allow mistletoe to be cut with a golden sickle as it was so precious.

THE YULE LOG

Cutting and bringing home the Yule log was a major occasion in big houses during final few days before Christmas. iStock

The Twelve Days of Christmas, which included our present New Year's Day and Twelfth Night (6 January), were the perfect excuse for having a good time. Where possible, big family gatherings would be held or feasts where the servants as well as the masters would be entertained. Carols would be sung by the poor, and extra pennies collected to help them celebrate later on. A more boisterous variant on carol singing was the traditional wassailing. Wassail is an old English word meaning 'be of good cheer'. Poor people would walk round the parish singing wassailing songs either for money or, more usually, beer. Those who were better off might have in their possession a wassail cup, large and often of elaborate design, which they would fill with mulled beer or wine and use to toast each other. Mummers' plays – medieval morality plays – were also performed in many places. A traditional Yorkshire wassailing song began:

We've been a-while a-wandering
Among the leaves so green.
But now we come a wassailing
So plainly to be seen,

For it's Christmas time, when we travel far and near;
May God bless you and send you a happy New Year.

We are not daily beggars
That beg from door to door;
We are your neighbours' children,
For we've been here before!

In a custom dating back to Roman times, the roles of master and servant were overturned on one day of the year around Christmas time, with the staff served a feast by their employers. Sometimes a Lord of Misrule might be appointed from among the servants – a kind of fool king. In some military regiments even today the officers serve Christmas dinner to their men. Another charming custom was to lay the table for two on Christmas Eve, to welcome Joseph and Mary on Christmas morning. There was also a superstition that animals were able to talk on Christmas morning, and some people, particularly children, would creep to the pens and cowsheds as the sun rose in the hope of catching them doing so.

Yorkshire folk followed the ancient tradition of first-footing, by which the first person to cross the threshold of a house on I January should be male, and should bring a nugget of coal (signifying warmth in the year to come), a coin (for prosperity) and a piece of cake or bread (for plentiful food). In some parts of Yorkshire the first-footer should have dark hair for extra luck – but in Skipton it was regarded as bad luck if a household's first-footer was a redhead. Finally, it was also traditional to celebrate New Year's Day with a party, reflecting the universal belief that it is lucky to begin anything in good spirits. Of course, this tradition still holds true today.

I wish you a happy Christmas and a happy New Year,
A pocket full of money and a cellar full of beer,
And a good fat pig to last you all the year.

Mistletoe, an unusual plant that is a parasite on other trees, is now closely associated with Christmas but at one time it was venerated by the Druids.

A YORKSHIRE MISCELLANY

Finally, Yorkshire has its own collection of customs and traditions, all of which contribute to the characteristically rich and vibrant place we know today. Here are just a few of them!

Food and Drink

The most characteristic food served in Yorkshire is, of course, Yorkshire pudding. In its home county this batter pudding is traditionally served as a starter, rather than as part of the main course as is more common in Sunday pub carveries nowadays. In days gone by huge slabs of Yorkshire pudding would have been served as a first course, soaked in gravy and the juices of the roast beef which would have been cooked above it – in the days when meat was the most expensive item in the diet, the batter pudding served to fill up hungry people and make the meat go further. Indeed, in poorer households the cheaper pudding might have formed the only course, perhaps served with dripping instead of gravy. Still, an old Yorkshire proverb notes:

Them as eats t'most pudding gets t'most meat.

Parkin is the other well-known Yorkshire delicacy – a cake made of oats, flour, fat, ginger and black treacle. It is baked to a dry

Yorkshire pudding, served as intended — on its own, with plenty of gravy! iStock

consistency, but with storage it softens and becomes sticky. It was traditionally common across most of northern England, but in West Yorkshire in particular it has become inextricably associated with Guy Fawkes Night, when it is eaten around the bonfire along with baked potatoes and treacle toffee.

Folk Remedies

In the days before the National Health Service, rural folk had to rely on the services of local healers to remedy their aches and pains, or else fall back on folk remedies or 'granny cures', as they were sometimes known. Yorkshire folk believed that warts, a common complaint, could be cured by stroking them with a snail, then impaling the snail on a thorn. Alternatively, the wart could be touched with a small piece of meat, which might then be buried to rot and somehow take the wart away with it.

If someone was bitten by a mad dog they might be given a church door key to hold, and amulets or talismans were often given to ward off evil spirits. Holy water from church fonts or sacred wells was given to people to drink, anoint themselves with or carry in phials, and plants were often employed to treat specific ailments – such as juice extracted from willow bark to treat fevers and headaches, which is now known to contain salicylic acid. This has similar properties to aspirin!

Sheep Counting

In days gone by, shepherds had their own systems for counting their woolly charges. These counting systems probably descended from Celtic languages similar to Welsh or Cornish, and they were used at the start and end of every day, and after any action that involved moving sheep – for example, from one pasture to another.

These system are known collectively as 'yan, tan, tethera' and are known in different versions from around Britain – but uniquely in Yorkshire the system was also used for knitting, as preserved in a 'knitting song' passed down through generations. The knitting count up to twenty goes like this:

"Yahn, tayhn, tether, mether, mumph, hither, lither, auver, dauver, dic. Yahn-dic, tayhn-dic, thether-dic, mether-dic, mumphit, yahn-a-mumphit, tayhn-a-mumphit, tether-a-mumphit, mether-a-mumphit, jigit."

Lyke Wake Dirge

One of the most famous English folk songs, the Lyke Wake Dirge, was recorded in Yorkshire dialect around the fourteenth century. It is a funeral chant that would have been sung over a corpse (or 'lyke') during the traditional wake before burial, outlining the hazards and trials of the soul's journey from Earth to purgatory.

The soul must pass over Whinny-muire (thorn-moor) and then the Brig o'Dread, but the journey will be made easier if the recently deceased has engaged in charitable acts during their life. Verses describe the hazards of Whinny-muire are as follows:

This ae nighte, this ae nighte,
(Refrain) Every nighte and alle,
Fire and fleet and candle-lighte,
(Refrain) And Christe receive thy saule.

When thou from hence away art past
To Whinny-muire thou com'st at last.

If hosen and shoon thou ne'er gav'st nane,
The whinnes sall prick thee to the bare bane.

The song has been recorded by many artists over the years, from Pentangle to Jethro Tull, and the traditional melody has been adopted into the classical canon by composers such as Benjamin Britten. It has also given its name to the Lyke Wake Walk, a 40-mile challenge walk across the highest and widest part of the North York Moors National Park.

iStock